I Wish I Were Beautiful

Jasmine Tiedemann

I Wish I Were Beautiful

tellwell

Tellwell Talent
www.tellwell.ca

ISBN
978-0-2288-5846-1 (Hardcover)
978-0-2288-4601-7 (Paperback)

To Brantley and Lily
I hope you can always find the strength
to believe in yourself.
But if you can't,
know that I will ALWAYS be there
to pick you up.

Lately, I've been having this feeling
that kind of makes me sad.
I've been wishing I could look different,
but thinking that makes me feel bad.

I don't really feel pretty.
I don't even feel cute.
It seems I'm always getting
stepped on by somebody's boot.

Getting crushed to the ground is awful.
It makes me feel so small.
Mom, I want to tell you ...
I wish I were beautiful.

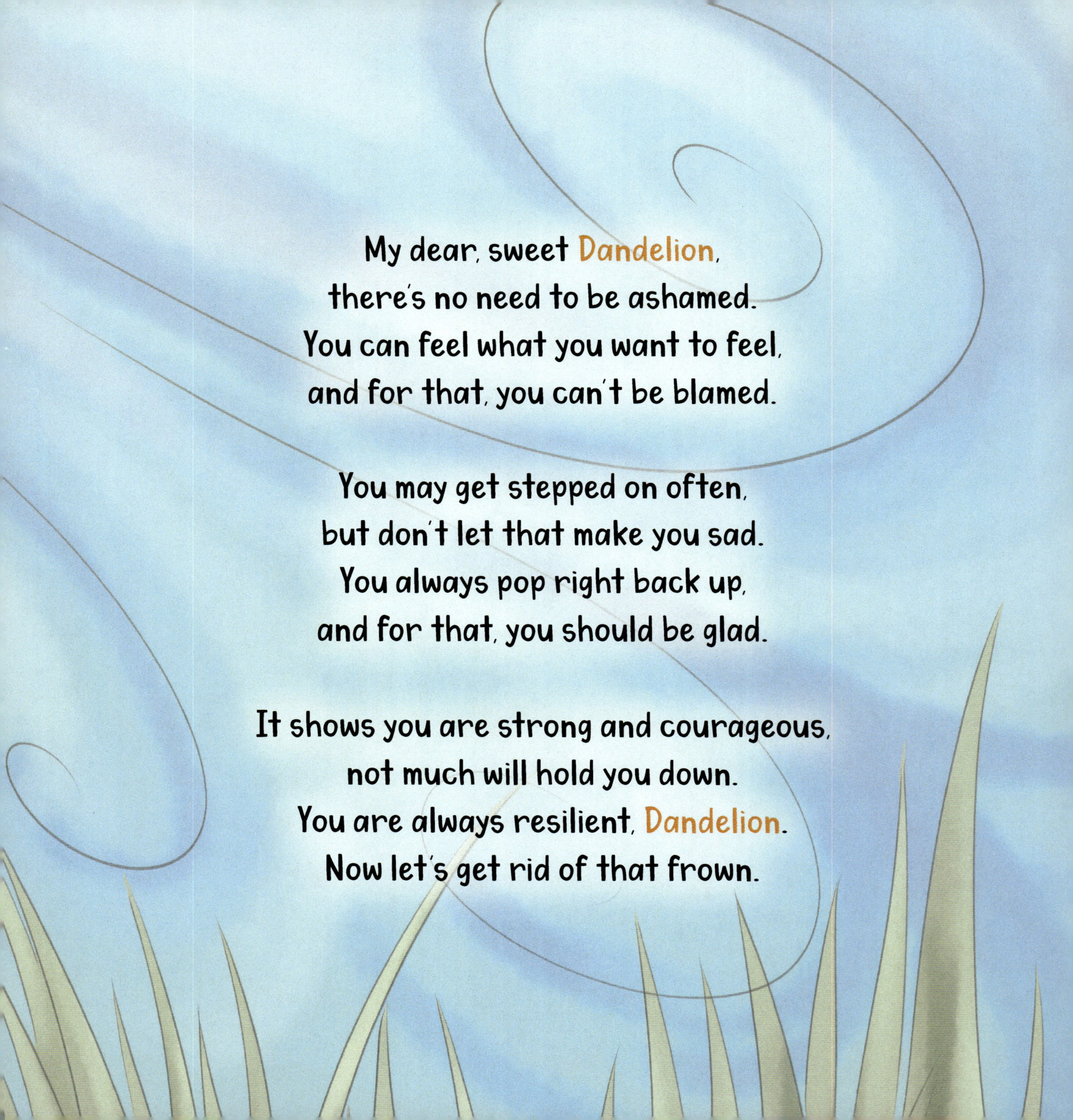

My dear, sweet Dandelion,
there's no need to be ashamed.
You can feel what you want to feel,
and for that, you can't be blamed.

You may get stepped on often,
but don't let that make you sad.
You always pop right back up,
and for that, you should be glad.

It shows you are strong and courageous,
not much will hold you down.
You are always resilient, Dandelion.
Now let's get rid of that frown.

But Mom, I wish I had
beautiful long petals, like Tiger Lily,
instead of these short stubs.
They make me feel so silly.

And I'm only one boring colour,
call it yellow, amber, or gold,
not a rainbow like Petunia.
I wish I were that bold.

But, Dandelion,
in this big sea of green,
you will always stand out to me.
Why would you want to look more like them?
When you are the prettiest flower I see.

Yes, your petals are quite short.
It's what makes them cute and fun.
And one colour is not so bad,
for yours is as bright as the sun.

Mom, I wish I were planted in a garden,
like Tulip and Sunflower.
I could grow big, strong and beautiful,
like a blazing tall tower.

Instead, I'm forgotten, cut down,
called an ugly invasive weed.
Pulled out like an intruder,
in a garden I have no need.

My beautiful Dandelion,
what would you have to gain
from being planted in a garden?
Would you want to be contained?

You are vibrant pops of yellow
and downy balls of seeds.
You grow wherever you choose.
You get to be wild and free.

I crave to stand out like Snapdragon.
I wish I looked more unique.

And smelled as good as rose
I want my petals to be that sleek.

Instead, I smell like nothing.
I look just like all the rest.
And when winter comes and I'm dead and gone,
I will definitely not be missed.

Dandelion,
just open your eyes.
You are more amazing
than you could ever realize.

I understand there are a million
who look just like you,
but look up to the stars
in the big dark blue.

A million wondrous specks of glitter.
Now, don't you see?
In our simple patch of grass,
we make up our very own galaxy.

You Dandelion are unlike any other,
so tell all your doubts goodbye.
Make a wish, believe in yourself
and one day you will fly ...

About the Author

Jasmine Tiedemann is a photographer and a stay at home mom. She loves to take pictures of anything and everything but her favorite thing to photograph is flowers. She shares her love of books with her children and spends too much time at the library. She currently resides in Leduc Alberta with her husband and two kids.

Manufactured by Amazon.ca
Bolton, ON

19890958R00019